Book Writing; Fuzzy about Where to Start?

by Connie Dunn

A Teaching Book

Printed in The United States of America

January 2012
    10 9 8 7 6 5 4 3 2

Library of Congress Cataloging in Publication Data

Dunn, Connie
        Fuzzy about Where to Start to Write Your Book?

Writing
        Fuzzy about Where to Start to Write Your Book?
        by Connie Dunn

Publishing
        Fuzzy about Where to Start to Write Your Book?
        by Connie Dunn

Education
        Fuzzy about Where to Start to Write Your Book?
        by Connie Dunn

NOTE: This page is the copyright page. Please note the parts to this page. It is not necessary to understand it all but these pieces should be found on your copyright page. We will look at the items on this page in a later section of this book.

For Nancy Cantor and the Dream Factory Community
for encouraging me to use my expertise and long history
with writing and publishing to help others
who wish to write with coaching and writing support groups

For all writers

For my wife, who supported me through this project

For my daughter, Michelle, who is my best editor

For my daughter, Erin, who was my best student

NOTE: This page is the dedication page.

The role of a writer is not to say what we all can say,
but what we are unable to say.
~Anaïs Nin

A word is not the same with one writer as with another.
One tears it from his guts. The other pulls
it out of his overcoat pocket.
~Charles Peguy

Table of Contents

NOTE: This is an important organizational piece for your book. In some ways, it is the briefest of outlines. Many of the books made for Kindle, Nook, and other e-readers do not use a Table of Contents. I believe their reasoning is that you aren't giving page numbers, which are a normal part of printed Table of Contents. However, those books that I've previewed that do have a Table of Contents have links to those Chapters, which makes a quick way to find the information you are after.

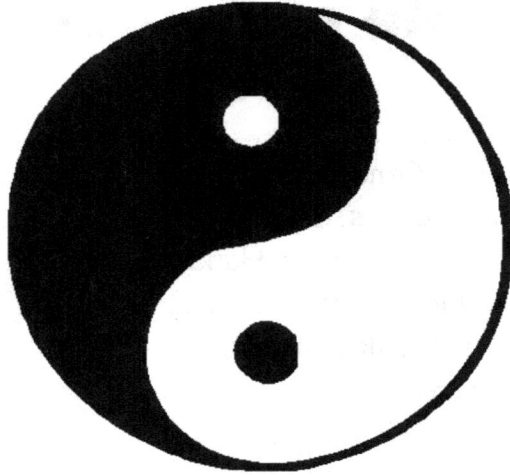

Like the Yin-Yang of Eastern Religions, writing is a balancing act. On one hand, you want to be creative. On the other hand, you need to structure your writing in a manner that your readers can easily get your message! Whether you are writing non-fiction or fiction, you have a message or purpose in writing the particular book that you are writing.

Introduction

It is my hope that this book will help people to write their own book. It's been many, many years ago now, but I can almost remember my first introduction to self-publishing. I had been writing for literally years, and I had written a cookbook, which I self-published. But I did not have a guide for publishing a book. I'm sure I made a lot of errors. I was running a writing group when I had been contacted by a woman who wanted the opportunity to talk to my writer's group.

A beautiful Black American woman stood before my writing group. I don't remember what her name was, the name of her book, or any of those details. But what is very clear in my mind is how knowledgeable she was. She sold a booklet that discussed self publishing. She touted her book as a best seller.

A lot has changed in the publishing world since then. Printing was done by offset press not printers from a computer. All the text had to be typeset and built onto a page. The pages were assembled, printed, and bound.

What has changed is that the formatting is now done on the computer, usually by the author. If you have an agent or a publishing company, you may not get that involved in these processes. However, more and more people are self-publishing.

There are a lot of famous authors who have self-published, so don't let people tell you that if your book was worth publishing, a publishing company would take it on. Did you know that e e cummings' <u>The Enormous Room</u> was originally self-published? The most popular book on styles, <u>The Elements of Style</u>, by Strunk & White was also self-published before it was picked up by a publisher. Did you know that Richard Bach's <u>Jonathan Livingston Seagull</u> was rejected 140 times prior to final publication and Margaret Mitchell's <u>Gone With The Wind</u> was rejected 38 times?

According to go-publish-yourself.com, "authors who self-publish are having success like never before. Internet marketing, e-book publishing and social networking sites have helped self-published authors get their books in front of potential readers and book buyers. The playing field is becoming more even. When you self-publish, the control and success of *your* book is in *your* hands."

Rejection is something that must be endured by authors who go through established publishing company routes. For example, Stephen King's <u>Carrie</u> was rejected 30 times; <u>Chicken Soup for the Soul</u> was rejected about 140 times and <u>Harry Potter</u> by J. K. Rowling was rejected by approx. 12 publishers. The road to publishing has been a hard road and depended so much on others. Agents were one of the best ways to get published only a few years ago. Today, it is difficult to even get an agent, and getting an agent that actually has connections to publishers is yet another hurdle.

You may find these statistics interesting: According to self-publishingresources.com, women buy 68 percent of all books published; it takes an average of 725 hours to write a non-fiction book and a mere 475 for fiction; and a recent survey showed that 81 percent of the people surveyed said they felt they had a book in them.

There are some very good reasons that any writer should consider self-publishing. First and foremost, publishing companies get so many manuscripts that your manuscript may never get read. If you want to get your book out quickly, this is definitely an obstacle. "Technology is turning mass markets into millions of niches, according to self-publishingresources.com. "Independent presses, self-publishers, and authors can sell effectively into these micro-markets. This bodes well for new and mid-list authors, not to mention creative-minded smaller presses." This website also reports that 78 percent of all titles (books) published are purchased from small publishers and self publishers. There are also from 8,000 to 11,000 new publishers appearing in the marketplace every year, the majority are self-publishers.

For self-publishing, there are a few things you need to learn about book design or book building. Some things are fairly standard and once you develop some wording you can use on other books you write, this is called "boiler plate." Learning the right words to use on your copyright page and what goes on the page are steps toward getting your book manuscript in printable format. In the following sections, I'll be giving you a lot of information about writing and publishing your book.

This is, however, not a book that teaches you how to write. Putting one word after the next in a cohesive manner is part of the writing process. While beginning your book can be done in a lot of different ways, you have to decide what method suits you best. I'm a linear writer in that I need to get my "title," maybe even the picture that I'm going to be using on the cover, before I can even write up my table of contents.

Not everyone writes in this straight line fashion from beginning to end. I've known people who write from the center of the book out. Others just start someplace and begin. I'm not sure how either of these writers gets a book written, perhaps because I do think and organize definitively from the cover. It does not mean that the story starts in the beginning. While I wouldn't have a clue how to start my book writing from any other place than the beginning, the actual tale or story that you tell may start midway. I don't want to confuse, but thinking linear in reference to the overall book and thinking linear to the story you tell are not one and the same thing.

A story often begins in the middle of things. It is usually told chronologically from where you begin telling the story. You see, the story needs to start whenever the action gets interesting. If you began the story when the person was born and painstakingly write all the details of their life up to the point where the action begins, your readers will likely not stay with you.

When beginning to write a book, I find that coming up with the title is my first step. Once I have the table of contents, I could start writing anywhere in the book, I suppose. However, I find it easier to write from the first word to the last word in the book. I go back over it. And from time to time, I find I've put a chapter or portion of a chapter into the wrong place, which requires some editing. Every writer needs some editing.

It isn't everyone's way to write. Some people literally write from the inside out. But to write in this spiral manner would take a different organizational technique. And I admit that I'm so linear that I often have to find artwork or create artwork for the cover before I can continue. This can be a problem in that the artwork may not reflect the entire book in the same way that waiting until the end to create it. But don't worry! It really doesn't matter if you write from cover to cover or from the middle out or even rectangular - whatever that would be – use your own best organizational style and thought processes to write your own book. It would be tragic for you to let the starting place stop you in your tracks! And that happens with a lot of would-be writers.

***Writing is a learned skill, so just about everyone can write. But not everyone does write. To be a writer, you need to actually do the work: sit down and put one word after another. Getting yourself organized to do a book means different things to different people. Just begin! It'll all fall into place.

In this age of electronics at our fingertips, people are used to writing in a type of code. For example, "cu" means "see you." Writing a book, whether it is a non-fiction or fiction manuscript, has to be written in good English or good American-English. While colloquialism or unique dialects do work in fiction pieces as you are using them to create characters; they also work into your non-fiction work when they match the people you have interviewed. These colloquial dialects should be kept at a minimum to make your book more readable, but using them can also add a dimension to your book.

```
I. Major Topic 1
    A. Topic 1-1
        1. Topic 1-1-1
            i. Topic 1-1-1-1
            ii. Topic 1-1-1-2
                a. Topic 1-1-1-2-1
                b. Topic 1-1-1-2-2
            iii. Topic 1-1-1-3
        2. Topic 1-1-2
            i. Topic 1-1-1-1
            ii. Topic 1-1-1-2
            iii. Topic 1-1-1-3
    B. Topic 1-2
        1. Topic 1-2-1
        2. Topic 1-2-2
    C. Topic 1-3
II. Major Topic 2
    A. Topic 2-1
    B. Topic 2-2
        1. Topic 2-2-1
        2. Topic 2-2-2
III. Major Topic 3
    A. Topic 3-1
    B. Topic 3-2
    C. Topic 3-3
```

← **Structure**

Structure →

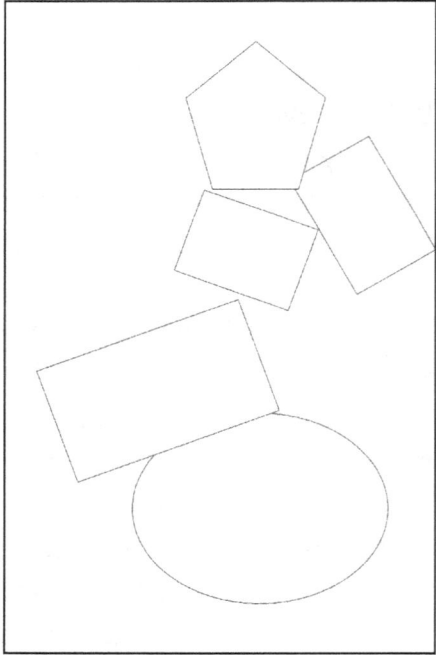

Outlines, Titles, and General Structure of Books

Outlines

Outlining may remind you of your school days. However, it can help you organize your book. Consider your major headings as Chapter Headlines and list all those Chapter Headlines to make up your Table of Contents. If you outline in this manner, then everything that comes under those headlines are sub-headlines in your chapter.

For example:
The following is the Table of Contents, but modified to show it in outline format.

I.   Introduction
II.   Outlines, Titles, and General Structure of Books
III.   Agents, Publishing Houses, and Self-Publishing
IV.   Interviewing, Research, Proper Handling
         of Quotes, and Plagiarism
V.   Dedication Page vs Thank You List;
VI.   Preface and Introduction
VII.   ISBN Numbers, Libraries
VIII. Book Covers and Book Design
IX.   Formatting and Editing
X.   Writing Habits, and Writing Styles
XI.   Pictures and Copyrights
XII.   Copyrighting Your Book
XIII. Promotional Quotes

XIV. Marketing Your Book
XV.   Biography

What you put under these chapter titles will help shape your chapters. This simply helps you think harder about how each chapter will be shaped. Many authors, including me, only go to this point with outlining. However, let's take this chapter, for example.

A. Outlines, Titles, and General Structure of Books
   1. Outline
      a. Using the first level of outlining as chapter titles
      b. Using the second level of outlining as sub-headlines within the chapter
   2. Titles
   3. General Structure of Books
      a. Title/Cover
      b. Inside Cover - Blank Page
      c. Dedication Page
      d. Copyright Page
      e. Table of Contents

Titles

Titles of chapters can either be informative or so intriguing that it pulls your reader into the chapter. While the Title of your book is far more important than your Chapter Titles or Chapter Headlines, as a writer, you need to pay attention to these details.

One of the best resources for checking out titles or headlines to see if it will be received the way you wish is the Headline

Analyzer, located on the Web at:
http://www.aminstitute.com/headline/. This is a free tool,
which is provided by the Advanced Marketing Institute. What
it does is measure the emotional marketing value of your words.

As a wordsmith, maybe you already know that some words illicit
certain emotions in people. There is a list of "magic" words that
are highlighted in NLP (Nuero Linguistic Programming) that our
brains are pre-programmed to be more receptive.

MAGIC WORDS

ADV/ADJ	AWARENESS	SPACE	TIME
Easily	Aware	Expand	After
Naturally	Realize	Beyond	Now
Unlimited	Experience	Before	Because

See how easily we can help our readers expand their brain!
Because the magic words flow naturally, your readers will
realize a higher level of rapport with your writing. The trick, of
course, is to do this so naturally within your writing that no one
will realize it.

Titles and headlines should, however, go with what you put into
the paragraph(s) that follow. If you don't, it will cause your
readers to be repelled by your writings and may not pick it back
up.

Needless to say, you should take care in what you write. You
don't want to deceive your reader. Nor do you want to turn
them off. It depends, of course, in what genre that you are
writing the journey in which you take your readers. And think of

the headlines (title) and sub-headings as road signs on the map that outlines the whole journey.

General Structure of Books

Books have a fairly standard structure: **Title (cover), Blank Page (or inside cover), Dedication Page, Copyright Page, Table of Contents.** Then, on the next *Right-Hand Page*, the first Chapter or Introduction begins. Chapters should begin on right-hand pages. Go back over this book and check out these pages.

The even pages are what we refer to as the **Back** of another page. It physically lands on the *Left-Hand Side* of an open book. Since our eyes normally go to the right-hand side, that is where chapters should begin. Even if we need to leave a blank page between the end of one chapter and the beginning of the next, this is the industry standard of printed books.

Technical books also follow this format, even to the point of putting "This page intentionally left blank" on blank pages. I've always thought that was somewhat of an oxymoron, since it isn't blank now that you've put something on it.

I often fill blank pages with quotes or pictures when it seems to fit the intention of the book. I know that white space is something we should incorporate in designing pages, but somehow a whole empty page just seems to scream, "Fill me!"

Title/Cover

The Title Page or Cover is the very first thing anyone sees. On the Title Page, you want the Title, Sub-Title (if you have one), Author(s), and Illustrators (if there is one). If you have an illustration or photo for the cover only, you do not give illustrator credit. You should add this information to the bottom of the Copyright Page or if there is no room on that page, which often there is not, you can add it to the Dedication Page at the bottom. The main thing is that you give this person credit somewhere. However, if you purchase a Stock Photo from a stock photo site, such as Dreamstime (www.dreamstime.com), there is no need to credit anything. Giving credit is important; however, stock photo companies do not always give you the photographer's or illustrator's name. There is no need to credit the stock photo company. Do not just pull pictures off the Web from anywhere! That is plagerism!

Inside Cover - Blank Page

This is generally blank. In fact, unless you are creating an e-book, the page is logically blank, because it is the back side of the cover.

Bastard Title

The Bastard Title is a duplicate of your cover in most cases. However, the main pieces of the cover need to be repeated. I usually repeat even the picture, but often the formatting is different, because the cover design is something you do at the very end of creating your book.

What happens when you create your file for an on-demand printer that offers an online creation of the cover from templates is that you don't create the Bastard Title. You create a Title Page. This becomes the Bastard Title in your finished book.

Copyright Page

The Copyright Page is always on the back of another page or a left-hand page. In some books, the copyright page is on the back of the dedication page. Either place is correct.

The Copyright Page may be the most difficult to create for first-time book authors. However, after you've created one, you can copy and paste to following book projects and alter whatever needs to be different, such as the obvious: the title.

Let's take the Copyright Page piece-by-piece:

The very first line includes the title and who owns the copyright, which would be the author(s). Note that it is very unusual to copyright to a business rather than the person.

The next line is the publishing company.

Published by Nature Woman Wisdom

The next line is sometimes more confusing for self-publishers. The Edition refers to the number of times you have printed the book. In terms of on-demand printers, this is the first version of your book. Most of the time, you will see that a book is a First-Edition. However, popular books are often reprinted.

First Edition. Printed and bound in the United States of America.

With conventional publishers, the book is printed with a certain number of copies. Books destined for best-sellers would be printed by the thousands or even a million. If these are sold out, a reprint is done. The litmus test of changing editions of the book is whether it is run from the same type and same publisher it remains the same Edition. When a book is published by a different publisher and/or different type, meaning the media used for printing, it then becomes the Second-Edition.

Printing methods have changed drastically within the last 100 years. Printing from moveable type has not been used for quite some time. But even within the last 40 to 50 years, printing has changed dramatically and become so much easier due to computers. We now can do everything typesetters used to do right from our keyboards. Therefore, printing it is simply a matter of getting that file to the right sort of printer...then, we can print the book in a matter of minutes where it used to take literally days to print and much longer to set all the type.

Our next line or section of the copyright page is to explain your copyright terms. I know it may seem redundant, but this is a very important. Perhaps, we just need to explain it for all those folks who just don't get what copyright means. This should be worded similar to what I have below.

Following the copyright terms, we repeat the year of copyright and the name of the person holding that copyright. Followed by the ISBN Number, the Publisher, and the country where the book is printed.

Copyright © 2012 Connie Dunn
ISBN-13: 978-0615587882
ISBN-10: 0615587887
Published by Nature Woman Wisdom

Please notice that there are actually two ISBN numbers here. ISBN stands for International Standard Book Number. The reason for the two numbers is logical: ISBN-10 was used prior to January, 2007 and ISBN-13 thereafter. The ISBN-13 is your 13-digit ISBN number. The ISBN-10 can be found within the ISBN-13, which basically adds the 978 prefix and a check digit at the end of the number.

The 13-digit ISBN is expected to accommodate a growing demand for numbers around the world. The ISBN is used to identify a particular title and edition and specific publisher, which is used for marketing by book distributors, booksellers, libraries, universities, and wholesalers.

The next section on the copyright page is fairly easy to discern, it shows where the book is printed, the month and year, and what edition. The edition is shown by the number or numbers not shown in the series. In this case, 1 is not listed. If this were a second edition, then 2 would not be shown.

Printed in The United States of America
January 2012
10 9 8 7 6 5 4 3 2

The rest of the information on the copyright page refers to the cataloging in the Library of Congress. What this section does is make it easy for libraries to catalog your book. You should put every conceivable topic that your readers might look up when looking for your book or a book with the same or similar information.

Library of Congress Cataloging in Publication Data

Dunn, Connie
        Book Writing: Fuzzy about Where to Start?

Writing
        Book Writing: Fuzzy about Where to Start?
        by Connie Dunn

Publishing
        Book Writing: Fuzzy about Where to Start?
        by Connie Dunn

Education
        Book Writing: Fuzzy about Where to Start?
        by Connie Dunn

Dedication Page

The dedication page is a fairly straight forward page. You simply include the names or groups for which you dedicate your book.

Blank Page

A blank page will follow here, because the dedication page is always a right-hand page. You can put some other information here, quotes, a picture, or anything relevant to your book. If you haven't found a place to give credit to the person who took the photo or drew the picture that you are using for the cover, this would be a good place to do that. It usually is found on the bottom of a page. So even if you have nothing else on the page, you put this credit on the bottom or close to the bottom of the page.

Table of Contents

The Table of Contents is just that: a list of all the contents of the book, which is organized by using chapter titles and includes the page number where the chapter can be found. If you list not only the chapter but also sub-headings within each chapter, you should list the page for each.

Agents, Publishing Houses, and Self-Publishing

Agents

Agents or Literary Agents, to be specific, help you get your book published. They work for a percentage of your royalties and/or advance, depending on the agent and their contract with you. Naturally, some agents are better than others. When you hire an agent, you want them to take your book to publishers and sell the book and you. A good agent should have relationships with many of the publishers for the genre of your book manuscript.

As a general rule, agents should not charge reading fees. However, you may have to evaluate on your own, because most sites allow agents to list themselves, which means that the site, itself, doesn't endorse the agents.

You can find lists of agents at places, such as http://www.writers.net or http://www.firstwriter.com. When you find an agent on a list, you receive limited information. One way to feel a bit more confident about specific agents is by searching their name in Google or some other search engine. This should bring up comments or information for authors who have worked with the agent. The best way to get an agent is to get a referral from another writer, but if you're a new writer you might not know other published writers with agents. And some writers are not willing to share their agent information.

Agents not only represent you and your book to publishing companies, they also help you develop as a writer offering constructive feedback. They don't get paid unless they can sell your manuscript. Their feedback may reflect publisher's guidelines or current needs. An agent should know what the publishers are looking for, because a good agent will have a relationship with the people who make acquisition decisions.

For the large publishing houses or publishing companies, agents are almost a requirement. Otherwise, your manuscript is not read. Even those who publicize that they are taking unsolicited manuscripts may not ever get to your manuscript.

Publishing Houses/Publishing Companies

There are a number of ways to find a listing of publishing companies. Here's a few: http://www.searchforpublishers.com; http://www.publishers.org/; and http://www.acqweb.org/. Indie Publishers are somewhat new on the horizon, you can find out more at http://www.findyourpublisher.com.

You can send query letters to publishers, but normally sending your entire manuscript is a quick way to end up on the bottom of a very large pile. Indie Publishers, on the other hand, wish to partner with their authors. This translates into that you need to invest in your book.

Self-Publishing

Self-Publishing differs from Indie Publishers in that the Indie Publishers are partners in your published book. There are costs for both self-publishing and publishing through an Indie publisher. In defense of self-publishing, the stigma of self-publishing has lessened over the last few years with the arrival of e-books. These are easy to create and convert to.pdf (portable document file) that is readable across computer platforms. You can use freeware software programs, such as Calibre (http://calibre-ebook.com) to change the formats into Kindle, Nook, and other formats. E-books are the least expensive to create, because no printing is involved on the creator's part. With on-demand printing, you can print a run as small as one, so you can have a print format.

The newest arrival on the scene of published e-books, of course, is the Kindle, Nook or other E-Readers. Books can easily be converted into these formats. This is also a fairly inexpensive way to get published, especially if you have some expertise with formatting in these platforms. Unfortunately, each one uses a different platform. Kindle has now made apps for iPads and iPhones, so that may be a good place to start. There are also books available to help and many more service providers who will convert your book into one or more of these formats. The fees vary widely and depend heavily on the number of pictures you have in your hard-back or paperback book!

Marketing

Marketing is one of the largest pieces to publishing a book. It's one of the places where most authors have difficulty. I know I do. I enjoy writing, but marketing can be arduous and time consuming. It's easier to jump to the next writing project.

There is quite a lot of information about marketing your book online. For example, http://www.bookmarket.com/; http://tribalauthor.com/; http://www.iuniverse.com; http://www.writersservices.com/wps/ pr_marketing.htm; and other sites have good information and tips on marketing your book. Whether you self-publish, go to an Indie Publisher, or get published by a major publisher, you will need to do some marketing yourself, if not all! There are some schools of thought that viral marketing is a fairly easy way to market your book. There are no easy methods, but viral marketing is definitely a great choice in selling books. Using social media, you have opportunities to reach a wide audience.

Depending on your reason for publishing your book, the publishing options and marketing become clearer. If you are a speaker, publishing a book can give you a credential and give you something to sell at your speaking engagements. Speakers should also consider CDs and other materials that support their speaking.

Interviewing, Research, Proper Handling of Quotes, and Plagiarism

Interviewing

When writing a book, you may find that interviewing others and including their comments will help your book and maybe lend more credibility to the book. Set up appointments to interview your list of interviewees, which could be authorities on certain topics you cover. If you are to meet them in person, dress appropriately. Business attire is usually acceptable in most situations. You don't want your interviewee to make assumptions about you based on your attire, so your purpose is to make them comfortable.

Recording their comments can be done several ways. Using a digital recorder is one way. Writing their comments down is another. I find that a combination of both works best for me. If you're interviewing via the phone, make sure to try out your recording device. There are many options using the Internet, as well, some of these sites automatically record. However, you can't control those as well as equipment you actually handle. Use what is most comfortable to you.

While most journalists will tell you that once you've told your interviewee what your intent is with their comments, anything they say is fair game. This works for some people, but I like for my interviewees to be happy with what I write and quote from them. If I'm unsure that I've captured that, I e-mail my interviewee with the quotes that I've captured. It gives them the opportunity to correct my interpretation of what I thought they've said. In the long run, I believe this gives my interviewee some comfort and gives me an assurance that what I publish is accurate.

Research

Just like interviewing, research can add to your book, depending on what you are writing. Doing research can take you into the deepest reaches of your local or regional library or even your closest University library. Some research can be done on the Internet. While the Internet is a wealth of information, a lot of the information is not able to be verified as accurate. I am an Internet junkie when it comes to research, but I do try to get similar information from more than one source. You have to use your own instincts about research just like interviews.

Proper Handling of Quotes and Plagiarism

Make sure to give credit to all people you've interviewed. Use quotation marks appropriately. When you use research information, make sure you've quoted that information accurately and given proper source information. You don't have to use footnotes or even give a list of resources at the end of your publication, unless this is an academic publication. However, it is important to give credit where credit is due. If you use a source for inspiration to write your own words, make sure you're really using your own words and not just rehashing what someone else has written. This can get into plagiarism. But for this to be an issue, someone does have to compare and take issue by going to an attorney to claim plagiarism. It can happen, so make sure you've done your due diligence. Remember, someone can take your material, as well. In fact, with the Internet so widely available around the world, it is possible for someone to take your information, publish it on their Website, and then claim you plagiarized their information. This is when copyright registration saves your bacon! You can prove when your information was written, can the other party?

The best advice I have is to register your manuscript with the copyright office as soon as you are finished with your writing project. The fee is only $35, which is quite cheap when you consider attorney (minimum of about $100/hr and most are now at $300/hr) and court costs (these vary from state to state and municipalities to municipalities.

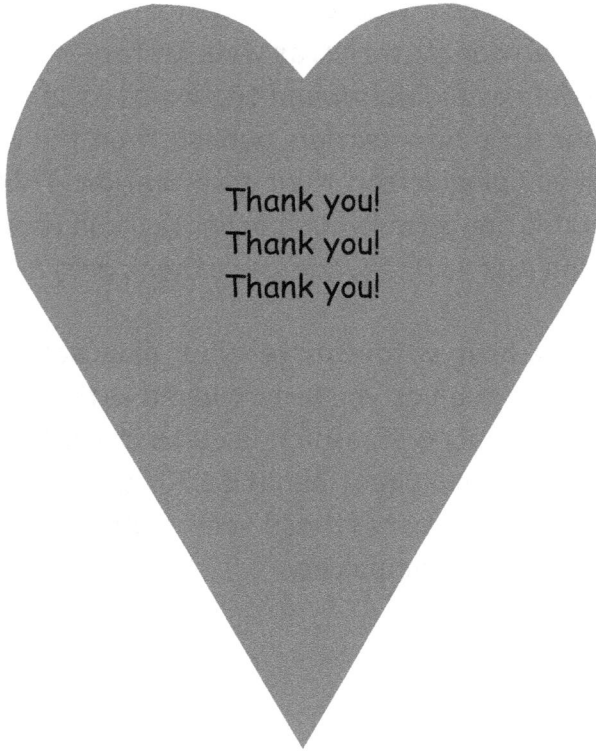

Dedication Page vs Thank You List; Preface or Introduction

Thank You List

The Dedication Page is not a Thank You List. It is appropriate to thank your contributors, when a book is made up of materials contributed, but this is not done on the dedication page. It is usually done after the copyright page or at the end of the book. Some people choose to thank people in a preface or in their introduction; this is appropriate use of these sections.

Preface or Introduction

A preface can be written by someone else as a way of introducing your book. You do not need a preface if you have an introduction, unless it is written by someone else. If you have a mentor or a friendship with a big named write or expert in your field, having them write a preface is a way to gain a bit of notoriety. Make sure you put Preface by on the Cover, so you can make the most of your relationship.

Dedication Page

Dedication Pages are a place to name a person or persons or group of people for whom you are dedicating the book. For example, I usually name my wife, because of her patience in putting up with my writing projects. I also mention my two daughters and possibly even my granddaughter, but most of all I try to dedicate my books to the group of people for whom will gain the most out of the book. For example, this book is dedicated to writers.

ISBN Numbers, Libraries

ISBN stands for International Standard Book Number. According to Bowker, "The purpose of the ISBN is to establish and identify one title or one unique edition of a title from one specific publisher. An ISBN allows for more efficient marketing and cataloging of products by booksellers, libraries, universities, wholesalers, and distributors."

ISBN numbers are important for your book, if you want to sell your book in such places like brick and mortar bookstores; Amazon; or get it into any libraries. The ISBN number is an assigned number gotten through the Bowker (http://www.bowker.com), which is the official ISBN assigner for the U.S.

While the ISBN becomes part of the bar code, the bar code is different to the ISBN. A bar code is simply that a code in bars that represents the ISBN number. You can purchase a bar code along with the ISBN number or you can buy software that will do that for you.

You can buy ISBN numbers in a singular or block fashion. More information is available on the Bowker Website and training courses are also offered, see http://www.bowkertraining.com/.

According to Self-Publishing Review (http://www.selfpublishingreview.com):

> *One of the major ways that mainstream authors sell books is to library chains across the U.S. Even if a*

traditionally published novel does not sell to the reading public, libraries can significantly make up the difference. There are over 16,000 public libraries, plus thousands more university and specialty libraries in the U.S., so this comprises a significant sales opportunity. Though libraries buy on a discount, let's say libraries buy a $16.00 self-published book for half price. The resulting figure is hundreds of thousands of dollars if the book is widely bought by libraries.

On the other hand, Self-Publishing Review says, "The same issues that hurt self-publishers in bookstores also apply to libraries as well. Though librarians are becoming more aware of the demand for certain self-published titles, the general consensus is that librarians stay away from self-published books.'

Don't let this discourage you from getting your book out into the marketplace. Creating a small press that prints only your book or going through a small press takes the sting out of the self-publishing, because then your book is not published by you but by a small press. There are a lot of ways to get around this "self-publishing" status. And depending on why you are publishing your book, the negativity of self-publishing may not even be relative.

If you are an entrepreneur and your reason for self-publishing is to offer your clients and customers a product, these people are not going to care if it is published by some major publishing company. You will! A major publishing company is going to offer you a small Royalty on each of the items it sells, but if that Royalty is under $5, which is likely, then it'll take a long time or a lot of books to make up any significant holdings. On the other hand, if you pay for on-demand printing for $5 or less and set your own selling price to let's say $20. Then you'd be profiting $15 per book. If you have lots of clients or your book is on a hot topic, you could make a good deal of money fast.

Let's say you've packaged a set of CDs to go with a course or workbook. If the cost for all of this is $20/per set, and you sell it for $300, then your profit is $280. You see where I'm going? Everything is relative. Your clients want your expertise, they don't care who published it!

For fiction and non-fiction writers of certain categories, the publisher may become an issue. Even still, take stock in your bottom line and how you're going to market the book. It all comes down to bottom line. If you want to publish your book, there is always a way!

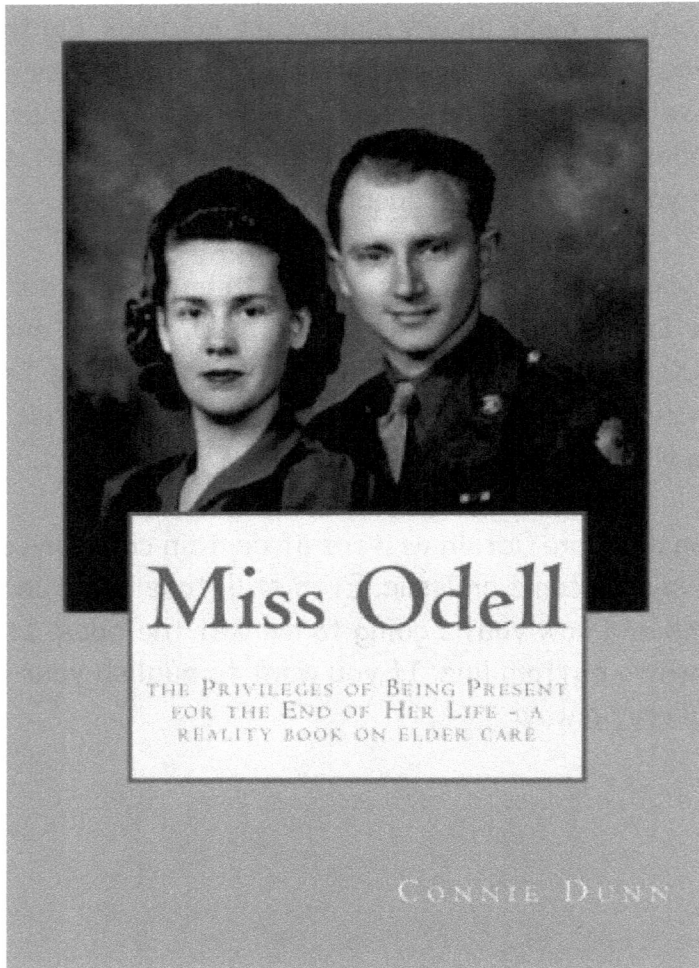

Sample of Book Cover

Book Covers and Book Design

Book Covers

As I've mentioned earlier in the book, I usually do start with the book cover. I find or create the perfect picture for the idea that I have. For me, it helps to see it visually to understand it more deeply. I am also a visual learner, so having the graphical representation for the cover helps me get through the book with the one idea. Each time, I begin a new book project, the symbol that I keep in my mind is the cover picture. So if I don't like that symbol, I probably need to pick one that I do like.

For example, the picture on the cover of this book is from Dreamstime.com, which is Royalty-Free and is one of their stock photos. I buy it as Royalty-Free, but I don't own the photo. Dreamstime can sell the rights to this photo over and over again.

I design the cover, which for me usually means selecting a font and the illustration/photo, and finding a good title. I use the help of the Headline Analyzer at http://www.aminstitute.com/headline/ to help me decide on a title that captivates. It is run through their analyzer to determine what percentage of appeal it has and analyzes intellectual, emotional, and spiritual aspects. There is a good explanation of what the analysis means on their Website, as well.

After the book is completed, I use a template on my on-demand printer site to further design the cover, which is also based on the size of the finished book. So, my initial design usually becomes the Bastard Title page and part of the interior pages that are formatted to the size of the finished book. Page breaks have to be adjusted for the completed book size.

Book Design

Once the book is finished; the entire book is then converted into a .pdf before uploading. Let's think about other design items that you may have noticed in other books. All of these need to be chosen before you convert to a .pdf. For example, some books are written in two columns, have subheadings in all the chapters. Technical writing usually numbers the pages and the paragraphs. This makes it easy to find what you're looking for, but isn't really standard for most genres.

You may want to have a two-column page with illustrations inserted in the second column. This is particularly a good idea if you have a lot of illustrations that help explain your topic. For example, a book on construction of just about anything would benefit from accompanying illustrations.

Some of these design elements can be thought of in advance and created as you write, others don't lend themselves to this and need to be added at the end. Charts and tables can be done as you are writing, but they will have to be reformatted and may even have to be redone completely to fit into your page. If you choose an 8 ½ X 11 finished book, then less reformatting will have to be done. We generally write in such programs as Microsoft Word™, which has a default page size of 8 ½ X 11. The easiest way to format your book in a different page size is to choose a non-standard page size on the Page Setup menu, go to the Paper tab and choose the parameters you wish. You can choose for your pages to have margins or bleed over the edges. I don't know how the pages would look without margins; I would be concerned that words would be falling off the edges. However, you can play with it to see how it looks.

The most popular book trim sizes are: 5 X 8 inches; 5.25 X 8 inches; 5.25 X 8.5 inches; 6 X 9 inches. Industry standard book trim sizes are: 5.06 X 7.81 inches; 6.14 X 9.18 inches; 6.69 X 9.61 inches; 7 X 10 inches; 7.44 X 9.69 inches; 7.5 X 9.5 inches; 8 X 10 inches; 8.5 X 11 inches.

Font and size make a difference in clarity.
Jont and size make a difference in clarity.
Font and size make a difference in clarity.
Font and size make a difference in clarity.
Font and size make a difference in clarity.

Font and size make a difference in clarity.

Font and size make a difference in clarity.

Font and size make a difference in clarity.

Font and size make a difference in clarity.

Font and size make a difference in clarity.

Formatting and Editing

Formatting

In the previous section, I talked about formatting as it pertains to the overall design of the book. That is a huge part of getting your book ready for printing. But you also want a good book!

Formatting also pertains to typeface, the font and size, which you use. If you use a very elaborate font, it could make your book too difficult to read. If you make the font too small, you can't read it! Headlines and subheads within chapters or sections can add to the readability or make it too choppy, so it is both a design and formatting decision you need to factor in.

Formatting a book needs to take the reader into consideration. For example, for children's books, the type is usually larger than in other books. These are generally picture books, so only a line or two may end up on a page.

Page size and margins contribute to formatting decisions. If you've chosen a very small trim size for your book (let's use the 5 X 8 inch trim size as an example), then the size of the font and margins are going to make a big difference in what your book will look like. See illustration on left.

When choosing a typeface or font, most people go with either a sans or non-sans font. An example of a sans font is: Sample. An example of a non-sans font is: Sample. Notice that there are slight differences in the two fonts. I am using Comic Sans font, which might be a bit fancier or have a slightly more stylish look than the Ariel. The Times Roman is a very standard font. It has the marks on the edges of the T whereas the Ariel does not have T.

Some people feel the sans fonts, like Ariel give a more crisp look to their book. Choosing fonts is strictly up to the Book Designer, which for Self-Publishing is you! This could be another reason for self-publishing.

Editing

The key to creating a good book is to make sure it's readable. If there are a lot of typos in the book, that distracts the reader from reading, then you have failed to produce a quality book. To make sure, hire an editor or copyreader!

You can hire an independent or freelance editor to read your book or you can have a friend read it. Friends, however, tend not to be good at telling you that you need to rewrite sections. They don't want to hurt your feelings. The result, of course, is that you put out an inferior product.

Some people can edit their own work. I have a problem doing that. Because as I read the manuscript, I read it as I intended it to be written. I never see the errors. I have a good editor, my oldest daughter. She is available most of the time, although she does have a 2 $\frac{1}{2}$ year old at the time of this writing, who can sometimes keep her mommy from working, she has managed to edit my materials. She knows how necessary it is!

Writing Habits, and Writing Styles

Writing Habits

Writing habits are important to develop. I'm not talking about the words you put down on your pages, such as in bad writing habits of using wrong punctuation or something like that. What I'm referring to here is developing a discipline or habit of writing. Set aside time to write.

Setting aside the time in your schedule helps, but you may also need to set goals. You may need an overall goal of when you want to finish your book. Picking your birthday, anniversary or just an arbitrary date sometimes helps you reach your goal. Having an accountability partner is also helpful. I'll talk more about this near the end of this section.

If you can, set aside at least an hour per day to write. It works best if you set aside the same hour every day. I love to write, so I sometimes have to set aside time for other things in my schedule. If you're writing a book, create a goal of writing so many pages. For example, if you write one page a day for an entire year, you're going to have 365 pages. That's a good size book in today's market.

If you are writing a book to bolster your credibility in your field, it's likely that you can write a much shorter book. For example, a friend of mine is a productivity and marketing coach.

He wrote a book that was maybe 35 pages. It's not a big book; it's probably more of a booklet. What this book did was establish his credibility as an Internet Marketing coach. He gives the book away on his Website as an e-book, but it is also on sale as a printed book on Amazon. It is a self-published book, of course, but this does not make it any less potent to his clients.

Self-publishing is a quick way to get your book into your niche market. It is a viable and lucrative means to publishing for many entrepreneurs, especially in today's market of instant access to large amounts of information.

Accountability

As a writing coach, being an accountability partner is one of the services that I offer. But you can have other people serve in this role. Probably the best way is to partner with another writer. That way, you can set up weekly meetings to make sure you're both staying on track. I have an accountability partner, who helps me meet my overall business goals. We serve this role for each other. We set weekly goals and send them to each other via e-mail. Then we talk each week to see how each other did. Just knowing someone is going to ask about your goals keeps you working on them.

Writing Styles

Writing Styles refers to the style of writing you use. For example, I tend to write from a personal viewpoint, using the word" "I" or "my" within my books, as I've done here. This is considered to be informal and would not fly as an academic book, but my niche market is not academia. My niche market is primarily entrepreneurs who want to write a book either to give themselves a credential or just to impart some knowledge to their own niche market.

What other styles are there? Well, not all styles are defined. Academic books use a much more formal writing style. This sort of style works well for many people. You write in third person and use very formal, structured writing.

If you are writing a novel, you need to figure out who is telling the story. If it is from the viewpoint of one of the characters, this limits what is happening with other characters, because you can only use what this one character is going to see and hear. However, if you have multiple viewpoints in a book, it can get confusing. Writing from a third person point of view gives you the autonomy to know what is happening with every character, including what they think. This is very popular with novelists. On the other hand, mystery writers like the one character viewpoint, because it can build suspense.

What writing style should you use? This is personal. If you are a new writer, you may not have developed your own style yet, but over time you probably will. When I first started writing professionally, I was a journalist, so I wrote in a more formulated mode using third person. When I wrote poetry even as a child, I wrote from this personal and emotional place. I took part in a psychological study at the University of North Texas where we discussed the psychology of our writing. One of our exercises was to figure out from where did we write? Did we write from the brain, heart, or other body part? I don't remember my outcome as much as the process of inner examination. You might try this. It may help you develop your writing style.

Because I like to write like I talk (only a bit clearer since I can think more when I write), my style developed into this personal style. It works for me, but it may not work for you. And I have to admit that I often veer away from this style when I am writing children's stories. But children's stories may only be three to five manuscript pages long, so there isn't a lot of room for adding me into the script.

Different genres may have different styles; you don't have to stick with one. Some writers write under different pseudonyms (by names). This is sometimes a good idea, depending on your name. Many famous authors used pseudonyms, so they could switch between editors and maybe even publishing companies. There are policies at many publishing houses that prevent writers from publishing more than a certain number of books per year. For prolific writers, like me, this allows them to develop maybe 10 or more pseudonyms from which to write. I've never done that, but my daughter, Erin, is in the process of writing Romance Novels, so she will write under a pseudonym. She's undecided about the name at this point.

For each pseudonym, she can develop a new writing style. The writing style is all about voice. Don't obsess over this. Your writing will evolve into your own perfect writing style. When I first began to write, I didn't have a style. I developed one over time. You can choose a view from which to write that seems to fit; and this is part of the writing style. People say that I write like I'm just talking to them. It's an easy way to write for me. And evidently it's an easy way to read! It works for me, but it may not be your writing style.

One way to see how other people write is to take their book and begin typing in their text. As you type, you begin to pick up on rhythm and other style pieces. Some of those pieces might include the voice, which is different from the viewpoint, because it incorporates a bit of the writer's personality. It also depends on what it is you're writing and the audience for which you are writing. Not only choices of words, but syntax or sentence structures, are part of your style.

Picture copyright © Connie Dunn

This picture was taken in the Great North Woods of
New Hampshire. There could be a million similar pictures.
But what is important about this picture is that I know
I took this picture and did not download it off of
someone else's Website

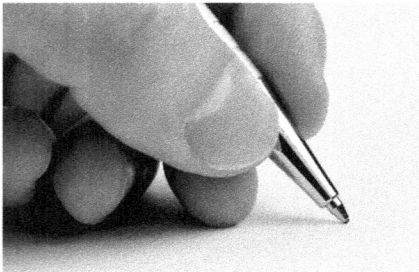

The picture on the left was
used on page 4. I did not take
this photo; it is from a stock
photo company on the Web,
called Dreamstime
(http://www.dreamstime.com)

Pictures and Copyrights

Pictures like the written word are copyrighted. It means that you cannot just grab some photo on the Internet and put it out there into the world as if you had taken it. You don't even have to label it for it to be considered as part of your copyright. This is okay, if you have gotten permission to use the photo. In that case, you may need to label it as such. However, getting photos from one of the sites that sells the rights to a photo means you don't have to label it or give it a disclaimer. There are a number of stock photo sites on the Web. They pay photographers for their photos and charge you a small premium for the right to use the photo.

When you need the disclaimer is when you've taken a photo from an individual or organization that is not set up for selling you copyright permission. You need to get permission, save the e-mail or letter so if there is ever a question you have proof that you got permission. All you have to do is show: "Source: organization or individual" or "Permission from organization or individual."

FYI: Whenever you use a photo that isn't yours, you should have permission, even if you are just using it in your newsletter. I know people have a tendency to just grab a photo, but that is plagiarism, because you're passing it off as if it was yours and you didn't take the photo.

Most people are willing to give you permission!

Clipart is another option that requires no mention of the source or permission. Some programs also include photos within the royalty free drawings.

While there is a possibility that you take a drawing or photo and modify it to the point that it is no longer the original, then you can claim it as your own. There is some gray area here and I would certainly tread on the side of caution.

The drawing on the left can be found on page 44. It falls into the category of clipart, but it is actually a combination of icons that have been made into fonts. The creation on the left can then be considered original, because each of the items are individual drawings.

There is no need to defend its originality, however, because it is covered under royalty free clipart. If for some reason, you use someone else's drawing, combining it with other drawings (clipart or another drawing of yours or someone else's) does not necessarily create a unique drawing. Modification needs to be to the point that the original drawing is not identifiable.

The picture on the left incorporates three separate items; however, combining three items doesn't necessarily create a unique picture. You can easily identify each separate picture or drawing, so the litmus of altering the picture/drawing did not occur.

Copyrighting Your Book

To copyright your book (Note: it also applies to audio recordings, musical works, sculptures, pictures, graphics, architectural designs, and other creative works), you simply have to have created it. There is no longer a law that applies to Copyright Notice, so this is not necessary in order to claim that it is copyrighted.

The confusion is in the difference between Copyright Notice vs Copyright Registration. There is more information about the laws posted on http://www.copyright.gov/circs/circ1.pdf. Please note that this is an official government site. There are a lot of sites out there that only want to take your money. The only official Copyright Registration site is on the copyright.gov site. Here's the link for books, including fiction, non-fiction, poetry, compilations of information, computer programs, textbooks, and similar printed materials: http://www.copyright.gov/forms/formtx.pdf. These works can be published or unpublished. More explanation is included on the form, as is directions about what should be included in each section.

For example, some sites want as much as $189 to copyright your material. But if you look carefully, there is a disclaimer that the US Copyright Office charges only $35, but it is written in very small type and easily overlooked. There is a whole package that they offer, but most of it is not needed. For example, within the package, they add things like copyediting, electronic record of the registration (you get this automatically from the US

Government), sample Cease and Desist letter (this would only be needed if and when someone challenged your copyright), customer support, and handling all your correspondence with the Copyright Office (if you fill out the form accurately, there shouldn't need to be any correspondence). When you need an attorney is when someone challenges your copyright, which is pretty rare unless you've actually plagiarized someone. Titles aren't copyrightable, so if someone has the same title on their publication –there really isn't anything you can do about it and vice versa.

Copyright Registration is a step you should take to protect yourself, but remember it can only verify the date for which you completed your form and paid your copyright fee online or via mail. There are other options for registering specific materials:

- Screenplays can be registered at http://www.wgawregistry.org/webrss/.
- TV Scripts, Concepts, and Screenplays can be registered at http://www.creatorsvault.com
- Christian Copyright help in getting licenses from copyrighted material for performances or to create copyrighted CDs, DVDs, and other materials, can be found at http://www.copyrightsolver.com or http://www.ccli.ie/ and there may be more of these sites. NOTE: This is somewhat different to original works, but is still information that might be relevant at some point in your writings.

Using passages or poems or other materials from previously published material is allowed. However, you need to make sure that you have permission to use the material and credit the source. There are some limits as to the amount of pre-published material from any one source you can use before it becomes plagiarism. There may not be any hard and fast legal rules or laws that govern the amount, but the intent is important. Are you trying to pass it off as your own material? Have you used quotation marks or indented and italicized longer quotes? If you need to use bigger pieces, you may need a license to use the material.

EXAMPLE: I used the following quotes on my book "Miss Odell: the Privileges of Being Present for the End of Her Life – a Reality Book on Caring for an Elder":

Part memoir, part love story, part field guide to elder care and services, this generous book offers the reader clarity, support and guidance around a tender issue. Connie's willingness to share her story, as she sits with her dying mother, blesses us with an experience of unforgettable grace and beauty. It is one that invites us to consider the precious gifts that come from embracing the end of life with an open heart.
　　　　　-   Cathy Jay

This book is a comforting end-of-life story, written by an unquestionably loving, caring daughter. Connie takes us on an enlightening journey, sharing her own personal story of living with, and then, letting go of her much-loved Mom, Miss Odell. She shares her personal story of the last days with her mom in a way that will bring peace to the reader, especially while sitting beside the bed of a loved one near the end of life.

Connie also covers many related topics such as, moving a parent to a new residence, care and services available to the elderly and working with all of the family members. A quick read that will help you prepare for the reality that we all must face.
　　　　　-   Maureen Monahan

Promotional Quotes

An important part of promoting your book is getting quotes from someone in favor of your book. I generally ask friends for this. I give them a preliminary copy of the book for which they can read and make comments.

Other sources would be book reviewers, newsletter editors (especially those whose audience includes people who would be potential readers), and professionals in the industry(ies) for which your book is targeted.

Getting the quotes is one thing, but using them is an entirely different thing. Using them involves creating effective promotional materials.

Promotional Materials

Brochures, flyers, press releases, and an assortment of other promotional materials can be used to promote your book. Events like book signings are popular and not only sell your book but give you an opportunity to meet and greet your readers. This also gives your readers an opportunity to get to know you.

Postcards, business cards and bookmarks are also good materials to support your events. These are giveaways that are directly related to your book and can actually include graphics of your book cover.

Press kits can include some of your promotional materials, as well as a photo of you, biographical information and your promotional quotes. Book cover replicas with synopsis, quotes, or various other information related to your book.

Building a Website for your book, including information about your book; you, the author; and any other information related to your book. If your book lends itself to activities, this is also a great way to attract people to your site. Facebook, Twitter, and other Social Media sites are all part of promoting your book.

Promotional Quotes can be used in all of the materials discussed here.

Getting speaking engagements surrounding the topic of your book is another way to promote your book and impart the important information for which you are passionate. How do I know you are passionate about your topic? Why else would you have spent time writing the book?

Marketing Your Book

Marketing is one of the largest pieces to publishing a book. It's one of the places where most authors have difficulty. I know I do. I enjoy writing, but marketing can be arduous and time consuming. It's easier to jump to the next writing project.

There is a marketing school of thought that says any product you develop needs a marketing plan. So when you've gotten that book in your hand, you've only done about half the job.

What good does it do to write a book, if you cannot get it to the people who most want to read it? The target audience might actually be best thought out prior to writing, so that you can gear your book to that audience. For example, if you're going to tell a story to a bunch of kids you would tell it a certain way. If you told that same story to adults, you'd tell it much differently.

The same goes for marketing. You market to your target audience. If you've written a children's book that teaches a value, your target audience is going to be parents who share that value. You need to know who they are, where you can find them, and what they need to hear in order to plunk down their cash for your book.

Once you know that, you simply write what those parents need to hear about your book into all your marketing materials, including press releases, brochures, and other materials. Then you need to get before this group of people to talk about your book, maybe do a little reading from the book, and have a book signing. This is often done in bookstores, but that may not be the best place for your book. Let's say your children's book with a value, valued how to care for a dog. Now, that opens up a larger number of possibilities for readings and book signings. Doggy Daycare, Pet Stores, Humane Societies, and other dog places are all good places to set up events.

Remember, too, that your first audience might be friends and family who have helped you get your book published in either explicit or non-explicit means. Hold a private party for this group and hand out books to them...these people will help with your word of mouth marketing.

Create press releases and send them out to appropriate sections of the newspapers you target. For example, if you book is about dogs, then the business section or real estate section are not going to be interested in this news release. However, lifestyle and possibly sections that feature pet owners might be. The more you get to know the publication, the better you will be at getting the right sections of a newspaper will be.

For example, my first book was a cookbook. My cookbook was featured in The Dallas Morning News' Sunday Magazine Cooking Section. They asked me to bake one of the desserts in the cookbook for which they took photos. I baked a peach cobbler. After all the photos were taken, the staff got to eat the cobbler.

I was interviewed, of course, and that all went into a story in the newspaper about my cookbook. During the interview, she asked where the cookbook was being sold and other details about how people could purchase it.

I only did local marketing, because it was before the Internet and my book did not have a barcode on it. Later, I purchased software that would generate bar codes.

There are so many easy ways to market your book now. First, create a Website and Facebook site. LinkedIn and other online communities are good, but they are mostly about connecting business to business, so it may depend on what product you are selling.

There is quite a lot of information about marketing your book online. For example, http://www.bookmarket.com/; http://tribalauthor.com/; http://www.iuniverse.com; http://www.writersservices.com/wps/ pr_marketing.htm; and other sites have good information and tips on marketing your book. Whether you self-publish, go to an Indie Publisher, or get published by a major publisher, you will need to do some marketing yourself, if not all! There are some schools of thought that viral marketing is a fairly easy way to market your book. There are no easy methods, but viral marketing is definitely a great choice in selling books. Using social media, you have opportunities to reach a wide audience.

Depending on your reason for publishing your book, the publishing options and marketing become clearer. If you are a speaker, publishing a book can give you a credential and give you something to sell at your speaking engagements. Speakers should also consider CDs and other materials that support their speaking.

If you're an entrepreneur, say a Productivity Coach, and you have a book on Productivity, it's understandable that the book will give you a bit more clout. You can choose to give it away or sell it. Either way, you outsource the printing with a print-on-demand printer. In this way, when people order, the books are printed and mailed. You just collect your royalty!

Biography

Connie Dunn is an author. She is also a writing, publishing, and creativity coach, who coaches writers from idea through published book. Self-publishing is Connie's specialty.

She is an educator with a long history of working as a religious educator for Unitarian Universalist churches. She also teaches creativity workshops, such as making magic wands and plaster masks. When artists, musicians, and writers hit a time when they cannot create, she helps them get over their obstacle.

Connie has a bachelor's degree in Marketing and Small Business Management. She has been writing all her life and spent more than 20 years as a freelance writer and had a regular column in such publications as The Dallas Morning News. This column earned her an award from the SBA for her work with Home-Based Businesses.

Connie is also a Certified Master Life Coach, Certified Master Neuro Linguistic Programming (NLP) Practitioner and Trainer, Master Reiki Practitioner, Vibrational Therapist (includes Color, Sound, Crystals, and Aroma Therapies), and Credentialed Religious Educator. She uses all her training to help people find their authentic self and their creative voice.

Other Books by Connie Dunn:

The Most Magical, Awesome, Delicate Creature of All (a new myth about how butterflies came to be)
Website: http://magicalawesomedelicatecreature.webs.com

Trees: Peaceful and Personal Meditational Poems
Website: http://www.trees-meditate.com

Goddess Rituals: Reclaiming Our Ancient Spiritual Heritage
Website: http://goddessrituals.webs.com

Miss Odell: the Privileges of Being Present for the End of Her Life – A Reality Book on Caring for an Elder
Website: http://www.missodell-realitybook.com

A Spider, Some Thread, and a Labyrinth Walk
Website: http://www.aspidersomethreadandalabyrinthwalk.com